Don't Take the Bait
Don't Become Offended

By: Dennis Paul Goldsworthy-Davis

Open Wells Ministries

15315 Capital Port

Sam Antonio, TX 78249

www.openwellsministries.org

DEDICATION

This book is dedicated to my wife who stood by my side during a time when I could have become so offended that I would walk away. She helped me on my journey through the battlefield of offense.

It is also dedicated to Dr. Gregg Marshall who was a dear friend during the most difficult time of my life and through whose friendship, and others like him, enabled me to overcome.

The battle was fought, the battle was won and now I share this book to help others.

OTHER BOOKS BY
DENNIS PAUL GOLDSWORTHY-DAVIS

Available on Amazon.com

Grabbing the Heel of Destiny

Grace Looks Good on You

Touching the God of Jacob

Standing in the Perfect Storm

Gaining the Commanded Blessings

Unlimited Anointing: Secrets to Operating in the Fullness of God's Power

Walking in the Prophetic

©2022 by Open Wells Ministries

No part of this book, written or graphic, may be reproduced by any means whatsoever, mechanical or electronic, without written permission from the publisher,
Open Wells Ministries, 15315 Capital Port, San Antonio, TX 78249

Library of Congress Number:

ISBN: 9798356186714

Printed in the United States of America by Open Wells Ministries

Scripture references were taken from:

THE HOLY BIBLE, NEW INTERNATIONAL VERSION®, NIV® Copyright © 1973, 1978, 1984, 2011 by Biblica, Inc.® Used by permission. All rights reserved worldwide.

KING JAMES VERSION

REFERENCES ARE PUBLIC DOMAIN IN THE US

Image on Cover by Freepik

Contents

By: Dennis Paul Goldsworthy-Davis

DEDICATION

OTHER BOOKS BY DENNIS PAUL GOLDSWORTHY-DAVIS

FOREWORD BY Chris Rodes

INTRODUCTION DON'T BECOME OFFENDED

CHAPTER 1

THE BIBLICAL MEANING OF THE WORD OFFENSE

CHAPTER 2

OFFENSES WILL COME

CHAPTER 3

HOW OFFENSES COME

CHAPTER 4

HOW DO I KNOW IF I AM OFFENDED

CHAPTER 5

BEWARE OF THE SIN OF CAIN

CHAPTER 6

TAKE HEED TO YOUR OWN SPIRIT

CHAPTER 7

WHEN YOU GO THROUGH THE WATERS

CHAPTER 8

HOW WE PASS THROUGH THIS PLACE OF WEEPING

CONCLUSION

BIOGRAPHY

FOREWORD
BY Chris Rodes

After almost 3 decades of pastoral ministry, I can say without a shadow of a doubt that an 'offended spirit' is one of the most deadly & heinous schemes of the enemy in the life of a believer! Unfortunately, on many occasions I have had a front row seat watching even good saints fall headlong into this pitfall of Satan. The inability to deal correctly with conflict, hurt, and offense has left numerous saints soured in spirit and in danger of losing their God-given destinies. I cannot overstate the importance of recognizing the trap of offense and rejecting it at any cost!

In this booklet, Dennis Goldsworthy-Davis exposes the sinister nature of this trap and how to defeat its workings against us as believers. Throughout its pages, you will find revelation and practical practices to defeat this evil trap of the enemy! Read this with an open heart and you will be armed to walk above the "snake line" of an offended spirit!

With almost 50 years of ministerial experience, Dennis gives wisdom from a seasoned, apostolic viewpoint. We, in the body of Christ, would be wise to heed the direction that fathers in the faith, like Dennis, give to us as they sound the alarm! "Walk with the wise and become wise, for a companion of fools suffers harm." ~ Proverbs 13:20

- Chris Rodes

INTRODUCTION
DON'T BECOME OFFENDED

There seems to be a new pandemic running through the Christian church! It seems to be fueled by the media and self-centered Christians who have forgotten that they themselves have been forgiven again and again. Unfortunately, they are so often not willing to forgive others. It is the pandemic of people becoming OFFENDED. Jesus himself warned us that offenses would come in Matthew 18:7-8, but 'TAKING AN OFFENSE, ' now that is another matter. This, as we will discover, is a pure choice that we make. We can be hurt, wounded, mistreated, and sometimes even abused. What we do with such things will determine the future of both our walk with God and also our walk with others. Nobody can avoid these situations because they are a part of life, but all can make a choice on how they can respond and deal with it. One of the toughest times in my life was dealing with an offense that nearly destroyed my walk and ministry. Another leader became offended at me and then others joined them in third party offenses. I then found myself responding in the same manner. God, in His grace, broke through to me and saved my ministry and my soul. It nearly caused a major nervous breakdown.

Have you ever heard the statement, "That's just plain unforgivable?" But unforgivable by whom? By you? By God? By whom? Sometimes we can become the judge and jury to a matter without hearing the matter fully. Years ago, I clearly remember being personally accused of something and a pastor writing to me and saying, "I cannot believe you did that!" He was right to not believe that I did it because I didn't. That pastor later found that out but was in danger of taking an offense over something that he didn't even check out. However, this was my answer to him. "It says in Proverbs 18:17, that the first to bring a case always seems right, until another answers him." I told him, "Even the law courts hear a matter out but seemingly not the church." Wow, how quick we are to form an opinion and take an offense without considering, praying, and looking for grace!

I pray that this booklet will help you. Written by one who has ministered nearly 50 years and has walked the many valleys of life!

CHAPTER 1

THE BIBLICAL MEANING OF THE WORD OFFENSE

In order to fully understand what it means to be offended, we must look at the difference between the Biblical meaning versus the modern meaning of the word.

The modern meaning, according to both Webster and Cambridge dictionaries, is: *to hurt the feelings of or to upset and perhaps even irritate and to cause to be annoyed.* This is totally different from the word in the Biblical sense.

The Biblical word used in the Greek for offense or offended is the word SKANDALIZŌ, from which we get the word scandalize. In Strong's dictionary, it means: *to entrap, that is trip up and stumble or to entice to sin and even fall into apostasy.* In Thayer's Dictionary it states: *to put a stumbling block, to entice to sin, to distrust and fall away from. To cause one to judge unjustly.* Quite simply, the enemy uses it to throw out the bait and see if we will take it. It can cause the breaking of relationships and walking away from and moving into other sins that connect to this 'Being offended.' They can be resentment, bitterness, and unforgiveness to mention but a few. In the worst case scenario, it can cause people to fall away from God and faith, according to Matthew 24:6. One biblical verse stands out here, Proverbs 18:19. "An offended brother is more unyielding than a fortified city" (NIV

1984). That means it is hard to break through such an offense.

We clearly must come to grips with the gravity of this ploy of the enemy and learn how to withstand it.

CHAPTER 2

OFFENSES WILL COME

It is Jesus who several times warned the disciples about offenses. In Matthew 18:7-8, He makes the statement, "Offenses will come." In John 16:1, He tells the disciples that He had informed them of all that would happen so that they would not, "become offended". As another rendering states it, "would not fall away."

So, Jesus himself warns us of the ploy of offenses. They will come but we must be prepared for them. We must learn how to combat them so that we will not fall for the ploy and take the bait.

Offenses will come, but we can choose whether or not to be offended. The simple words that are used so often now come into play. 'Take an offense! 'Just because a situation comes, and they will, it does not mean that we need to take an offense. When they hit us face on or side swipe us, the choice becomes ours on how we respond. Do we respond biblically with grace and forgiveness or do we choose to become offended? The choice is ours, but equally the results are ours to walk and sadly affect those who are around us.

CHAPTER 3
HOW OFFENSES COME

1. When God doesn't't act as expected

John the Baptist himself is warned not to take offense in Luke 7:23. Quite simply, John was in prison and was surprised Jesus hadn't broken him out. Which God did for Peter later on in the book of Acts.

2. Offended by revelation

Jesus watched many of His disciples leave Him when He revealed a truth concerning partaking of His life. This is found in John 6 and Jesus even asked the question in verse 61, "Does this offend you?"

3. When you offend yourself

In Matthew 5:29-30, we are clearly told the members of our body can cause us to sin or become offended. Yes, we can become offended at ourselves! Forgiving ourselves and having mercy on ourselves is often one of the toughest issues to deal with. We become harder and more judgmental on ourselves than the Bible is.

4. Trouble or persecution

In the parable of the sower, Jesus (Matt. 13:3-9 / 18-23) shares four different scenarios. One of those is being the shallow rooted Christian. He loves the truth and the experience, but has no root for when trouble comes. When it does come, it can be many times in multiple ways and manners. It can come at work, at home or at church. Here comes the offense, because shallow rooted Christians are so easy to pluck up and be caught in the wind.

5. By man

Now this is a big one! In Matthew 18, Jesus was referencing men causing even children to become offended. This can be men, rude men, arrogant men, unfair men and abusive men. The list can go on and on. Fathers, mothers, siblings, and pastors are all men. Quite often the ground of most offenses that will come will be mankind itself.

6. Circumstantial offenses

What is a circumstantial offense? It is something that happens outside of your plan. It can even be an accident or something outside of your ability to control. It could be you or a family member. It could be a child that goes astray or any other painful issue. Once again it throws us into a moment or choice of offense.

7. Preference offenses

One of my favorite Chapters in the Bible happens to be Romans 14; it is so full of gems. It covers becoming offended by others' choices on food, drink, special days, and even the way differing folks act through preference. It is a great chapter! Romans 14:13 shows us that in such choices we can offend or be offended. We must be careful not to let our preferences be any more than that, our preferences. This chapter tells us that we all live unto the Lord. So let's live to the Lord when it comes to preferences that are both ours and others!

8. Third party offenses

A third-party offense is when you take up an offense on behalf of another. It can be a spouse, a family member, a pastor, or a friend. The problem with third party offenses is that we never seem to get the whole story before joining the line of the offended. This must be avoided at all costs because often when the original offended person gets healed, the one carrying the third-party offense doesn't even know or has formed their own judgements.

CHAPTER 4

HOW DO I KNOW IF I AM OFFENDED

A better question is, "Did I take the bait?" Have I become entrapped? Are there signs? Yes, indeed. Your soul goes into prison. Psalm 142:7 states, "Bring my soul out of prison that I might praise your name." You literally fall away from God and man. You don't want to pray or be near God or His people and you become cold and indifferent. You blame others, but truthfully you know who it is.

Alongside the sign of indifference is not wanting to be around others, especially those who hurt you. We can have a lack of mercy toward others and are happy when you hear they are hurt, which sadly is a sign of vindictiveness and can often come under the word malicious. Clearly, now a root of bitterness has begun and is beginning to grow. Oh let's add, getting people on your side against the offending party. Hebrews 12:15 says that, 'A root of bitterness has now sprung up and wants to defile many!' Sometimes offended people begin to pray against others, thinking God is on their side. I remember doing that as an unsaved teenager against my own father. Offended? Indeed I was but when the Lord saved me he changed that spirit and later saved my father! That is what God is like! Not taking our side against another….

So let's look at the list:

- Cold and indifferent.
- Your soul is in prison.
- You fall away from God, which means you backslide.
- You fall away from people and fellowship with them.
- You distrust and form judgements.
- You become vindictive.
- You pray against people.
- You have a root of bitterness grow up (notice the word grow up).
- You want others on your side, which means you become a gossip.
- Maliciousness.
- You are offended easily.
- You are unforgiving.
- You want retribution.
- You want others to always come to you confessing their sins against you.
- You become narcissistic, meaning it's all about me.
- You lose your basic Christian ethos and become brutish.

These are just a few.

We have often said, 'if you don't deal with your issues, they will sure enough deal with you.' I have watched people backslide, become ill and sickly, have personality changes, lose weight and the opposite as they binge to hide their feelings. Asaph says some amazing things about it in Psalm 73:22.' I was senseless and ignorant; I was a brute beast before you.' Thankfully he found the antidote, the same we all need, before we dash our destinies and lives to the rocks. Never mind what we do to others.

Let's look for the signs and jump before they take root.

CHAPTER 5

BEWARE OF THE SIN OF CAIN

Who has not read the book of Genesis and been amazed by the actions of Cain toward his brother Abel, found in Genesis 4 verses 3-8? Both Cain and Abel brought offerings to the Lord, but Abel's offerings were accepted, and Cains were not. Cain becomes angry and offended and he is warned by God that sin was crouching at the door (verse 7). The first recorded offense had been taken and sin was waiting to have that door opened. THAT DOOR WAS THE DOOR OF OFFENSE. Offense, through jealousy! Cain opens the door and kills his brother. Look at the power of offense! He kills his own brother and becomes an outcast and loses his inheritance! (Genesis 4: 9-14)

We can become offended because someone else is more blessed than us. Offended because they get the promotion. Offended that God seems to be smiling on them. Offended because their ministry is famous and what about ours?? The sin starts with jealousy and becomes an offense, and the offense opens the door to the enemy. Then bang, here it goes! Cain is written for our example to show the power of a non-dealt with offense!

What is so sad about the story of Cain is that he was given an opportunity by God himself to fix it. The Lord speaks to him when he becomes offended. He gives him an opportunity to bring another offering and warns him that the enemy is waiting to pounce. 'Cain, don't open the door of offense!' 'Christian, don't open the door of offense!' Sin is crouching at that door and is waiting to have you and ruin your God given life. Cain falls into the ultimate sin of murder! To get to such actions he must have passed through so many temptations which were all fueled by jealousy and offense. We might not physically murder by shedding actual blood, but what about the killing of a reputation? What about hatred in our heart or maligning another all because we did not deal with the offense?

Sin (offense) crouches at our door! KEEP THE DOOR CLOSED. REFUSE TO BECOME OFFENDED!

CHAPTER 6
TAKE HEED TO YOUR OWN SPIRIT

God is speaking to the Israelite priests in the book of Malachi in particular. He has to deal with so much concerning them. From their giving to their attitudes and then also their desire to divorce. But in Malachi 2:15 NKJV, he warns them that their spirit was the reason they were acting the way they were. They had not watched their spirit and it had become offended; one could say that they had taken on an offended spirit. Undealt with offenses can so affect your spirit that it becomes an offended spirit.

Offended spirit? How would I know if I had that? An offended spirit is where one has allowed an offense to affect who they are, and it has now become part of their life and nature. They carry it with them! They wear it on their face, and it affects their personality. These people are not always very easy to be with. It's like watching someone who has sat on a thorn, and it won't come out. You see that in the movies where lions have a thorn in them and the affect it has. Jesus had to rebuke James and John, his disciples, and called them sons of thunder because of their spirit. In fact, he said to them, 'You do not know what manner of spirit you are of,' Luke 9:55 NKJV. Their spirit had been so affected and they didn't even know it! Do we know what kind of spirit we are?

Now added to an offended spirit, we can also take on a

spirit of offense. A spirit of offense is where our spirit has become so marred with the undealt with offenses, that everything becomes offensive to us. We become constantly offended by things and also by all things linked to or like what originally offended us. For instance, have you ever heard the statement, 'All men are the same!' All men? Including Jesus? The offense has turned into a spirit of offense and now any man can offend. I have seen this constantly with offenses against the opposite sex or pastors of churches and so on. One of the great dangers of this whole subject is that an actual demonic spirit can attach itself to our spirit because of the continual unforgiveness. As Jesus says so clearly in Matthew 18:34, 'This brings us into prison and delivers us to the tormentors.' This takes another kind of ministry to free us from this arena!

We must take heed when dealing with offenses that we watch our spirit and act quickly for our sakes and for those who are around us.

CHAPTER 7

WHEN YOU GO THROUGH THE WATERS

The book of Isaiah is no doubt one of the most terrific books on the ways of God. We are told that we will go through waters, rivers and fires in Isaiah 43:2, but the Lord says, "I will be with you." He says the same in Psalm 23:4 where He states that we are not alone during these times. His staff and rod, His comfort yet direction and discipline are there to help us through.

What does the Lord seek to achieve as we pass through these arenas of offense?

1. **He seeks to give us greater root systems as in Matt 13:21**

2. **He seeks to grow us up**

Hebrews 5:14 speaks of a maturity in Christ where God can entrust us with solid food and trust us to train others. James speaks of it in James 1:2-4. He tells us that maturity in God lacks nothing. Trusted in everything! Lacking no gift or blessing! Yes, grow us up Lord!

3. Enlargement in God

One of the greatest passages of scripture on going through offenses bring us to a place of enlargement, which means being of greater use.

4. Harvest of righteousness

Hebrews 12, you've got to love it. The disciples of God! Going through hardships and resistance and discipline, you cry, 'Really? 'What for? Hebrews 12:11 says, "…so that a harvest of righteousness will be produced in you." The nature and life of Christ is being produced.

5. To break the power of religion from you

In Matthew 15:12, the disciples let Jesus know He offended the Pharisees. Jesus' answer was, "Don't worry, my father didn't plant religion." If we have an ounce of religion, that I am better than you spirit or I do all my great works, then God is about to offend that thing right out of you.

We might pass through offenses, but that's what we must do. We must pass through and not get stuck in. "Pass through waters…" Isaiah 43:2. "Walk through the valley of death…" Psalm 23:4. "Pass through the valley of Baka (tears and weeping) …" Psalm 84:6. God will walk it with us if we let Him.

CHAPTER 8

HOW WE PASS THROUGH THIS PLACE OF WEEPING

One of the greatest of all passion psalms is Psalm 84 where we read of the love for God, the trusting of God and the journey toward Him! But, verse 6 is just fascinating. It tells us that on the journey is the place called Baka, the place of weeping. It was never intended to stop you, but was intended to cause us to overcome and find new wells in God that touch other people's lives. In fact, verse 7 tells us that we can go from strength to strength. Yes! Offenses can be our way into freshness of the Spirit and strength in God. How do we pass through?

1. **Have a "search me oh God" mentality**

In Psalm 139:23, the psalmist asks God to weigh his heart up and reveal it to him. That takes guts, but is a breakthrough prayer.

2. **Be prepared to be wrong**

The need to be right is actually a narcissistic attitude, a self-adulation that builds a throne for self. We must evaluate that we could be wrong, particularly in reaction.

3. Build forgiveness into your life and walk

Forgiveness has to be practiced and prayed and walked until it moves from blind obedience to a feeling of freedom.

4. Walk in accountability

Let others speak into you, correct you, and pray for you. They can help you overcome, especially praying that you can be healed of the offense as in James 5:16!

5. Be like Asaph

What did he do? When he saw his heart, he went into the sanctuary and sought the Lord until he got his answers! (Psalm 73:17) Force yourself back into the place where His presence is, where worship is, His good word and His saints!

6. Love covers a multitude of sin

This statement is found in 1 Peter 4:8. This is the guy who asked Jesus how many times he should forgive his brother. (Matthew 18:21) He found the answer. Put on Love! (Colossians 3:14) He found that by praying and practicing love, he became a man of love! Love covers a multitude of sins and will not hold an offense. Awesome!

So if entrapped, let's bring God in, His ways and His people. I know this works as I have lived it all and there has been His hand coming again and again!

CONCLUSION

Jesus not only said offenses will come, but also clearly told us that there would be an increase of them with the intention to cause even good folks to fall away (Matthew 24:10). We must be on our guard concerning this and not be so quick to take the bait. We must understand it is the ploy of the enemy to ruin our lives and testimonies and relationships. His whole intention is to cause us to fall away from our faith. That same insidious voice that said, "Has God said," is seeking to cause us to take the bait. He tried it with Adam and the last Adam and will continually try it with us. This booklet, I pray, will help us in our journey!

REMEMBER WE MUST NOT TAKE THE BAIT!

BIOGRAPHY

Dennis Paul Goldsworthy-Davis has been blessed to travel extensively throughout the world ministering both apostolically and prophetically to the body of Christ. He operates within a strong governmental prophetic office and frequently sees the Presence of God and the Spirit of Revival break out upon the lives of people. Dennis has equally been graced to relate to many spiritual sons throughout the earth, bringing wisdom, guidance and encouragement.

Born in Southern Ireland and raised in England, Dennis was radically saved from a life of drugs and violence in 1973. Soon after his conversion, he began to operate within his local church where he was fathered spiritually by Bennie Finch, a seasoned apostolic minister. After working in youth ministry Dennis pastored in several areas within the U.K. It was during these pastorates that Dennis began to see profound moves of God in these same venues.

In 1986 Dennis experienced a dramatic shift in his life and ministry. He and his family moved to San Antonio, Texas, to join a vibrant, functioning apostolic team. In 1990 Dennis was commissioned to start Great Grace International Christian Center, a local work in San Antonio. Dennis continues to serve as the Senior Minister of GGICC and heads the formation of the apostolic team in the local house. Presently, Dennis relates to several functioning apostolic ministries. He draws wisdom and accountability from Robert Henderson of Global Reformers, Barry Wissler of HarvestNet International and for many years, Alan Vincent. Each of these carry strong, well-seasoned apostolic offices in their own right.

Dennis has been married to his wife, Christine, since 1973 and has two wonderful daughters and four grandchildren.

Made in the USA
Columbia, SC
14 December 2023

27834487R00017